Stuph Like This

Stuph Like This

Etoya

Illustration by Briana Rice, Graphic Designer.

Xulon Press

Xulon Press
2301 Lucien Way #415
Maitland, FL 32751
407.339.4217
www.xulonpress.com

Unless otherwise indicated, Scripture quotations taken from the King James Version (KJV) – *public domain*.

Paperback ISBN-13: 978-1-6628-4016-6
Ebook ISBN-13: 978-1-6628-4017-3

PREFACE

The title and the contents reflect a collection of thoughts, events, ideas and emotions. Most of them were written to create an impressive image, take a stand or provoke a yet-to-be solved controversial issue. A few were written just for mere entertainment.

When one looks at a painting or other works of art, they begin to formulate words to express how it makes them feel or what image they see. "Stuph Like This," is intended to inspire, humor, relate to or formulate a picture in one's mind about what they read or hear.

A famous poet and commencement speaker at a college graduation was asked, 'What motivated her writing?' In that very moment, I began to ponder that question about my writing. My conclusion was, "stress." Love can be positive, peaceful or emotionally tormenting stress. Anger is usually negative stress but can be motivating to further a cause or show the comedy amidst some chaos. The variety of pieces reflect a presence, indifference and oftentimes an absence of stress.

The first poem, "If I Die Tomorrow," is the very first poem I wrote. It was written in one of the most stressful times in my life, so I thought. It is intended to inspire one to live life to the fullest. Our tomorrows may be planned but not promised.

COLLECTIONS

IF I DIE TOMORROW

If I die tomorrow
My death no grave defeat
For the life I've led
Will surely make
My obituary a mere receipt.
I was born a poverty-stricken child
Today called culturally deprived
And fought this insurmountable dilemma
To accomplish what others have tried.
Gone from church hymns to disco whims
From birth to acute adolescence
No more dependent or insecure
But an assured adult convalescent.
Sometimes a slow life, sometimes a fast life
At times reluctant with no ambition
Maybe a good life, maybe a bad life
Maybe a life of perfect mission.

Good times came in spatters
Bad times endurably long
Sometimes life's demands and pressures
Confused the right and the wrong.
Each moment was spent in full
With little time for leisure or rest
For I know without a doubt
I've seen life at its very best.
So, if I die tomorrow
All my debts and dues collected
If there's any part of life I've missed
With death I'll feel unrejected.

THE GREATEST THING

In stowed memories,
You've been tucked away.
And at times I am reminded,
Of the love in you.
One may want to know,
If love could be buried any deeper?
Is it love from the past
Or is it brand new?
In every verse and every rhyme
Is my life's story.
With so many pieces
One can easily read.
Your whispers echo in my soul,
And remain forever in my dreams.
I never knew,
Love could be stored,
As sacred energy.
That could stretch beyond
Any man–made boundary.
That every single moment
Was like sand in an hour glass of history.

TWELVE SENSES

He gives those who are truly connected
A sense of discernment
A sense of the supernatural
In dreams, a sense of prediction.

He also gives those who are truly spiritual
A sense of closeness and divine comfort
A sense of interpretation and intuition.
In time, a sense to see reality.

And then, to see reality beyond
A sense of awareness and beware-ness
And the recall of times long gone.
And so, be cognizant and cautious.

Fear is a cancerous creation that promotes
A sense of unknowing and beclouded deceit.
For He gives a sense of understanding
A sense of peace and the sense of joy
A sense love, strength and eternity forthcoming.
A sense of faith that only God employs.

UNCOMPROMISED DIGNITY

Real love is greater than just feelings.
Love is an expression of honor.
If the exhibition is reflective, then
Love is an expression of selfishness.

If the expression is selfishness
One is only able to honor themselves.
If one only honors themselves
They compromise the dignity of others.

This forces others to submit or concede
If one chooses to become submissive
There is a loss of self-respect and the
Respect of those who demanded the submission.

If one chooses to concede
Strength is renewed and revived.
Faith in one's self is restored.
Honor is reflective and dignity is uncompromised.

I STAND STILL

Do you really think
That I am so passive,
That whatever comes along
I will endure without any recourse?
I ache inside with so much anger
That my teeth grind when I am not sleeping.
I can hardly lift my cheeks sometimes.
In my most hilarious moments,
I Stand Still.

My eyes have been squinted so long
That medication can't rid my headaches.
Only the innocent elements of nature
Can alert my sense of feeling.
I am a mastermind of vengeance.
I will endure the impossible,
Documenting within my heart
While hoping it will return to you
But, I Stand Still
In anticipation of
A better day, a better world
A better way of erasure
And forgiveness for these feelings.
For He has eyes that see far beyond
The focus of small-hearted people
Dissolving my pain with reverence
When I grow tired of waiting on a change
I Stand Still, Until

AND THIS I PRAY

In my sleep
I am on the street,
And there, prayer has little clout
As I awaken, I pray
That right will still be right tomorrow
And wrong is long forgotten
That each day is filled with joy
Sterile of infectious past memories
And tainted hope for the future.
That our short-lived time on earth
Is productive and not filled with
Temporary indefinite ecstasies.
That the feelings I have nurtured between us
Do not betray me.
That God will show us the way to go.
That He will provide us with
The strength to make it
That we will trust in Him.
And not the echoes our bodies
And our minds.
That prayer tomorrow won't be
As lonely as it is today, I pray.

WHY

The youth disrespect their elders,
Adults don't treat fellowmen right.
Politicians obsessed with slinging mud,
And the next wars they're going to fight.

Do you hate looking over your shoulder?
Afraid to leave or stay at home?
For fear of being robbed or killed?
Not by others but by your own?

Our men are going to prison,
More women in the food stamp line.
Many leaders turning to drugs of choice
And smooth white-collar crimes.

The children blame the parents.
The women blame the men.
The men blame those other folks.
And the Christians blame it all on sin.
Socialists want to save the homeless.
Scientists want to save the earth.
Militias building new armies,
Preaching the denial of Christ's birth.
So why did God so love this world
That He would sacrifice his only Son?
Because he knows a better place
Than this old earthly one.

SOMETHING OLD

Why does the innocent look of yesterday
Seem strong, deliberate and lonely?
As if there is a hidden message now
Intended for just me only?

Why have soft touches turned to stone,
And gentle hugs into a firm pat on the back?
Holding hands suddenly seems juvenile,
And strong kisses are a short--short smack?

My cute steps and frisky turns
Use to highlight my way of walking.
New phases and invented pet names
Weren't suspicious terms of talking.

I can't stroke "ya now," with soft words
Or kiss an unfamiliar spot.
Cause the love for me has faded
And your heart has begun to rot.

SOMETHING NEW

Climbing to an altitude of over a thousand feet,
Seeking a space for a soft seat,
With the anticipation of a new love's clutches
Causing your heart to skip a beat.

The elevation and fresh mountain air,
All seem to synchronize with the setting sun
And the freedom of listening to nature talk
Is like a new life has just begun.

As stars sparkle all around me
Like a choir of life in perfect tune
This song will continue to chime silently
Under the direction of each new moon.

Love has found me once again
Over and over on the same face.
But this feeling in my heart is new
It just has a home in a brand-new space.

SOMETHING BORROWED
'A BETTER LOVE'

I sinned with you
Put my faith out on the line
And wallowed in Satan's mud
Like adolescent swine.

You gave me pain and sorrow
A smiling face with hidden tears
False hope and imitation love
Replacing faith with worldly fears.

How much I thought I loved you
Sometimes more than I did myself
How I put the love we had
On some high imaginary shelf.

But now upon another shelf
One higher than the sky above
Is the Word of Jesus Christ
And it is A Better Love.

SOMETHING BLUE

You may think that I've forgotten
The joyous times we shared.
My absences may have seemed to you
As though I never cared.

It takes some, more time than others
To gather the pieces and still go on.
With the hope that those who love them
Keep the faith while they are gone.

And during the time of healing
Many actions misunderstood.
Sometimes it takes an act of God
To change the hurt to good.

On many special occasions
I found cards well worth sending,
But none could nurture the loss of time
Of a heart that still needs mending.

THE LONG – HANDLED SPOON

Children,
    If you're always the one,
    Who's not having any fun
    And the joke always played on you?
    Ditch those snubbies
    And hatin' school buddies
    And feed them with a long--handled spoon.

Young People,
    If you are the only one
    Who never gets the 411
    Arriving too late or way too soon
    Don't pick up the phone
    Snap chat or go on Instagram
    Feed those friends a long-handled spoon.

Women,
    While out on the job
    You work with some-timey snobs
    Who go to lunch well before noon.
    Last to bring you a snack
    First to stab you in the back
    Feed them with a long-handled spoon.

Men,
    Relationships don't have to end
    Just get rid of some of your friends
    Like the ones who pour salt in your wounds
    Just give them some space
    Keep them out of your face
    Feed them too, with a long-handled spoon.

ASPIRATION

As the sign of the times would predict
Situations and consequences have aligned.
Awaiting compatible confirmation and
The invitation to swell internally.

For I've sown a seed, hence forth planted
In a tender bed of innocence.
And stand corrected on 'hap' magnetism
For it is truly uncontrollable.

Every day is absolutely different
In look, sound, smell and feel.
Constant environmental changes create
Premeditated grief for final days to come.

So, I shall live each day with every breath of self,
Embracing life as if nature could cease to exist,
And it shall, unless unclaimed passion
For aspiration is in the midst.

NEUTER GENDER

A scientist once categorized living things
By phylum, groups and species
But He sorted the living and the non-living
Theoretically fitting all the pieces.

One theory was that protozoa
Were neither animals nor plants
Maybe human beings shouldn't
Take a one-sided gender stance.

It's just another person's theory
Contrary to being either,
To purpose another hypothesis
Of possibly being neither.

Some people don't have a particular side
Categorized by a common mood
What some think is cute or sassy
Others perceive as being rude.

Some practice rules of gender conduct
At different phases of their lives
Like girls shouldn't soil their clothing
And boys should never cry.

What happens with equal hormonal levels?
For God makes no mistakes.
He created all existing life,
And man categorized the innate.

This doesn't have to be a radical change,
An uprising or revolution
Just think about adding a neuter gender
To the theory of evolution.

REACH IN, REACH OUT, REACH UP

This is for little girls, young ladies
And all women
Who have stayed away from God
And still are left with sin.
I know it's a hard battle
So, I'll tell you how to win.
Reach in your mind, reach in your heart
Reach in, Reach in Reach in.

But if you've turned away from sin
And know without a doubt
That you have been born again
And been cleansed from the inside out.
It's your job to get another
Steered on the Christian route
So, reach with yourself, reach with your faith
Reach out, Reach out, Reach out.

Now God is always looking down
On each one of us
Seeing if we'll keep the faith
When the going gets tough
And if our lives become hallow
Like and empty cup
He'll reach down and fill it with faith
If we'll Reach up, Reach up.

'Brethren, I count not myself to have apprehended, but this one thing I do, forgetting those things which are behind and reaching forth unto those things which are before.'
Philippians 3:13

SOFT SURRENDER

A midnight stroll
On some romantic strip
Is not as peaceful as
A walk on summer grass at dawn.
The sound of the ocean
Crashing upon the rocks
Does not come close to the melody
Of your whisper in my ear.
The soft glow of a full moon
On a foggy winter night
Has a much more perfect setting
Than music by candlelight.
There is nothing more comparable
Than the glow of your soft eyes
Or the gleam of your smile
That awakens my heart at sunset.
A multitude of hard-pressed passion
And surrendering softly to you.

STANDING

People these days worry too much about standing.
Standing all alone
Standing up too long
Withstanding
Understanding
Standing behind somebody
Standing beside somebody

Standing on the top
Standing under top
Standing in line
Standing in one time

But, no one wants to stand UP for much, like
Standing for freedom
Standing for justice
Standing for equal rights
Standing for love
Standing for choice
Standing for unborn rights.
Stand still sometimes
And patiently wait
Don't reach for things so near
Like random snap–chats
And Twitter feedbacks
Stand still till His will is clear.

I Samuel 12:16

NOMADIC SPIRIT

A man exists in the presence
Of his inner spirit.
And as he moves,
So does his spirit.

He that moves cautiously,
And in a complaisant manner,
Brings pleasure to
All tangible things.

He that moves
Hastily and recklessly,
Has an unstable spirit
And all things tangible are perishable.

An unrestful spirit,
Yields an exhausted
State of being
And all things tangible are unfulfilled.

WHAT IS IT LIKE?

What is it like to be saved,
But not Baptized in the in the Holy Spirit?
It feels like being cured
And not being able to feel it.

What is it like to be blind,
And not able to see?
It's like and abysmal prison
For which there is no key.

What is it like to be lame
And never able to walk?
Or having vocal chords
And never able to talk?

What is it like to be lost
To trod unfamiliar ground?
Just like most sinners
Whose souls are yet to be found.

It's like receiving the perfect gift
Never opening to see what's in it,
That's how faith alone is
Without receiving the Holy Spirit.

STRADDLING

I was caught up in the middle,
While straddling this old fence.
I couldn't win this war with self,
Cause I had no spiritual defense.

And I held that sinful fort
But ran out of ammunition.
I couldn't make up my mind
To forfeit sin and keep religion.

A cold chill ran all over me
And death gave my body a shake.
I knew at any given moment,
My soul Satan could take.

Right then I dismounted,
And surrendered my soulful pride.
Waved my true flag of faith
Vowing to stay on Jesus' side.

TRUE FORGIVENESS

At the moment of unforgiveness
You don't feel it when you say it.
You put your emotions on hold
Just long enough to fake it.

And then one moment after
You promise you'd forget it,
You wish you could take it back
Because you still regret it.

The next day gets even worse
When the guilt sets in.
To forgive and not forget,
Is still no lesser sin.

Pray resentment will escape you
And disappointments drift afar.
For the only true forgiveness
Is felt inside your heart.

SIMPLICITY

It is a safe state of being
And so easy to define.
It defends overt actions
When feelings are hard to find.

It's unlimited and unmeasurable
An uninitiated catchy phrase.
To those who strive on tangibility
A sequential continuous phase.

But a word is just a word,
And actions don't reflect reality.
There is no congruency or consistency
Between definition and the personality.

Complexity is more difficult
To label and to define
You can't tell what's going on
Inside a simple mind.

BALLAD OF DISTANT LOVE

In the beginning, God created,
The heavens and the earth,
The river beds and the surfs,
The lands and the seas,
The shrubbery and the trees.
The hills and the mountains,
The waterfalls and the fountains,
The domestic, the wild with their sting
But man came along and changed all these things.

As God stepped out in space and saw that, "It was good,"
Man stepped out on earth to change all that he could,
And the work that God put in creating Adam and Eve
Was changed overnight with Satan's power to deceive.
So civilization began along the Euphrates and the Nile.
Man was not content until he explored for miles and miles.
Even though God created all things below and up above,
He also created the abstract, faith, honesty, peace and love.
Believe in distant love and have faith that all the while
God created the gift of love but man stretched it by the mile.

KNIGHT DREAMS

His eyes so soft and serious
    A facial frame ever so strong
With a smile that enlightens the spirit
    Reassuring the right over wrong.
His chest of magnificent gallantry
    Sculptured like a work of art.
How can such a strong stature,
    House such a tender heart?
His arms to fold and caress
    Wrapping firmly with protection,
As emotions flow gently through them,
    They yield sincere affection.
Like the links in a perfect chain
    His hands to hold and guide,
Never in front nor in back,
    But always right by your side.
His nature of pride and confidence,
    Is much more than one could find,
For the knight who parades in my dreams
    Will forever be within my mind.

AN OLD FOOL

Don't open your sunroof on a clear night,
Cause an old fool won't see the stars.
It's not that he's lost his vision
He just doesn't want to focus that far.

To him the sunset has no color
It's not that he's color blind
He doesn't admire the scenery
Too much for a rusted mind.

Never changing his ways or his habits,
Has plenty excuses and backup reasons
He can't comprehend nature's beauty
Like a soul without a season.

He should bury himself in misery
Dig a hold about ten feet deep
Cause we don't want the children's eyes
Looking through and old fool's peep.

SURVIVAL

The content of one's character
Doesn't determine his fate.
Rather, stress is the contingency
Evident in what's innate.

The child who never cries
May not be the one who's stronger
And the child who's deemed the weakest
May not be who cries longer.

No life is safe and secure
Without the element of stress
Experimentation and problem solving
Are ways we take the test.

When we reach a peak of tolerance
A sense of reality sets in
And you make a determination
Of how you lose or how you win.

The means by which you do so
Is a choice only you can make
For the Geiger counter of survival
Is gauged by the stress you can take.

WHEN GOD WHISPERS

When God Whispers
You always hear it well
Above the traffic
Above the music
Above stories people tell.

When God Whispers
His voice is very dear
It's not a shout
Nor verbal spout
His message is very clear.

When God Whispers
You pause with gracious ease
You cease in motion
Decrease commotion
In preparation to receive.

When God Whispers
You recognize his voice
Only a second to verify
Another moment to clarify
Listening is not your choice.

When God Whispers
Like a melody of words
A soft sweet tone
When you're all alone
So He is sure to be heard.

After God Whispers
His words will never barge
Whether for yourself
Or for someone else
His message becomes your charge.

CHRISTMAS

All the land was silent
The midnight sky so clear
The stars seemed to dance in place
And twinkle a heavenly cheer.

God sent a Holy angel
From the realms of glory
To proclaim all over the earth
A never-ending story.

T 'was Joseph He first spoke to
Like magic it may have seemed
Because he did not wake him
But He told him in a dream.

That Mary had conceived a child
Much more precious than most,
For the child was not of man
But of the Holy Ghost.

That He shall have a name
Not like any one of us
That this holy child
Shall be named Jesus

And He should hold a special place
The highest among all men
For He is sent to this earth
To save us all from sin.

Joseph woke and took Mary
To the town of Bethlehem
And tried to find a place to stay
But there was no room for them.

The found a manager in a stable
And filled it full of hay
So Jesus would have a place
For his sweet head to lay.

Three Kings of the orient
Had come from afar,
Bringing gifts to the new King
As they followed the Holy Star.

And shepherds were in the fields
Attending to their sheep
When the holy angel came down
They rose upon their feet.

They were led to a place
Carrying their tokens of love
To receive God's greatest gift
That He sent from heaven above.

So each year at this same time
We show our love and care
With gifts that only represent
What He gave us all to share.

LEFTOVERS

It is wasteful to toss away
What could be saved for another day,
Just because it's what's remaining
And not needed for mere sustaining?

For ones who appear to be so needy
But self-evidence proves them greedy.
Accumulating unnecessary stuff
And glutting when they've had enough.

Trampling treasured moments like residue
Love and sharing long overdue.
Rambling and running and wasting time
Defying sacred vows that were once sublime.

Side-boarding slurs of unfound jealousy
Concealing the identity of the real enemy.
Casting those like mere throwbacks.
Withering relations that won't grow back.

There is a time and a place for old Casanovas
To remember the loyal and how you got over.
No more guineas, badgers and weekend gofers
Nobody wants your stale leftovers.

WHEN CHILDREN WHISPER

When children whisper,
What do they talk about?
Do they talk about children
That are their same ages,
Who lost their parents
And now live in cages?

When children whisper,
What a sweet–sweet sound.
Wonder what they really say
When we are not around?
Is it rudeness or disrespect
Or poverty and neglect?

When children whisper,
They hear profanity and inhumanity,
Hateful deeds and pure insanity.
Seeing that ignorance
Has taken center stage
And safe travel yields to road rage.

When children whisper,
They've paid close attention
To the gossip adults have mentioned.
That some groups should
Stay in their place,
And how they despise another race.

When children whisper,
They tell how adults tell lies
Of secret missions and foreign spies.
And how they don't give account
Of dirty deeds done
For the right amount.

When children whisper,
They tell about all their fears.
Of their hopes and dreams
For the coming years.
They talk about love and they talk about peace
And how the talk about war one day will cease.

MINDLESS

I close my eyes and become
lost within myself.
I can shut out the world
and go to a deep corner of my mind.
There, I can be alone or sad or cry.
It's the only place I can lick my
emotional wounds.
It's the only place I can love myself
for who I am internally.
I take care of myself here and
hold the spiritual hands of comfort.
I open my eyes to a different light and
a different sky every day,
never having the same view or vision.
To repetitive occurrences,
sunsets and sunrises are each uniquely
different every day.
Some views make my soul celebrate
and my heart dance
with so much beauty and unspeakable joy.

SLEEPWALKING

Some things in life are yet to be and maybe never realized. Some of us are fortunate to finally "get it" before we depart from this earth. One of the things I have learned is how to become a person of dignity and respect. The other thing is you can't lose what you never had. You can speed your whole life chasing a dream, fade into a nightmare and sleepwalk in someone else's dream. Sleepwalking is easier than coming to grips with the reality of failure to please yourself.

When the exterior self begins to unthaw, it awakens interior emotions that were clouded by trying to make someone else happy. You can finally feel yourself become human again from the inside out. You have fought the fear of dying in someone else's dream or nightmare. You have evolved to dream for yourself again.

BROKEN ANGEL

I can soar into a perfect sunset or glide with the rising sun at dawn but I am a broken angel with a broken heart and a broken spirit. I have tunnel vision with a blurred perspective of the future. It is not a physical inability to fly. It is a spiritual inability to soar.

I ask in prayer, I ask in faith, I ask in love that my heart be mended. Then, I can spiritually soar and my flight path is cleared. The strength of my wings will carry me forward into a restored vision of faith.

THE THIRD STRAW

The spirit of forgiveness is a powerful characteristic. It is both mentally and emotionally healing. The process is not taught but learned and lived. It aspirates the anger and the hurt and is held captive in the heart. When cured, it releases unspeakable joy.

The journey by which you experience the levels of emotional strife is measured in, "straws." For some people there is only one straw. It may be referred to as, "the straw that broke the camel's back." This phrase would imply that there were previous straws less painful. Therefore, the straws of hurt, harm or deceit are measured in degrees of human tolerance.

I believe that the first straw is, "shock." It is almost an unbelievable and decaying occurrence that is often soothed with tears of disappointment. The heart and mind work together to ease the pain of expectancy.

The second straw is, "deception." The second incident, although less shocking is equally hurtful because it was a revisited unfulfilled promise.

The third straw is, "anger," with yourself and others. The shame and guilt of expected deceit may be the final straw for most people.

"Fool me once, shame on you." "Fool me twice, shame on me." "Fool me thrice, and I am free." The number 3, in some spiritual texts, represents Devine wholeness, completeness and perfection. It is said to have positive affirmation.

EMPTINESS

The wills and the woes of living begins with the earliest memories of life. Mine centered on feeling rejected and alone at the age of three. I was never malnourished for food but starved for love, encouragement and a sense of belonging somewhere with someone. I felt empty. I feel empty.

When I opened my eyes for the first memory, I was sitting on a white dirt road in the front driveway of my grandparents' home. I was sobbing as I watched the cloud of white dust behind a shiny car fade away. I returned to this spot every day and cried behind the last memory of my mother. I felt empty. I feel empty.

I was the second child, the dark one, the one whose nickname was, "dusty." I had light brown hair and light brown eyes which had turned from dark gray as a baby, so I was told. I felt tainted to be compared to the sediment of colors and thus reflected my character. I was always dull and referred to as, "the other one." I felt empty. I feel empty.

When I awakened from this day dream was when my mother came to get me. I had been so untamable because I repeated my daytime routine of sitting in the dirt at high noon and crying after my mother until she finally came back for me. I felt retrieved but I felt empty.

After seven years of witnessing the horrors of mental, physical and emotional abuse upon my mother, the decision was made to return to the house behind the white dirt road to a life of emptiness once more.

I have come to know in life that emptiness is not always a state of containing nothing. In some spiritual beliefs, emptiness is an important door to liberation. For I feel full and I feel free.

MI MARIPOSA

Mija,

It's 4:45 am and as I peer through my cracked door, I notice your bedroom door is open and you are not there. For 18 years you have been cradled in that cocoon; listening, looking, dreaming, reading, watching tv, laughing, talking on your phone and many times crying when I was asleep and didn't hear you or sick and didn't call me. I don't know how many nights you have been afraid and didn't tell me but bared the fear alone.

As I write this, I realize that of all the gifts I could have given you, the one I am about to give has been dormant for 18 years. This migration for me this fall, will be the beginning of the present when you will have graduated once more. You will return to a future state that I have been preparing for you. It was your idea you wrote about friendship and the monarch butterfly that inspired me to complete this journey for you. We will always be connected in spirit.

As we migrate within our hearts, we find each other in prayer. I will forever await your safe return as God's guidance propels your wings of success. I will love and cherish the gift of your life from the edges of the earth onto the steps of heaven.

VALUES

Social media has unraveled the fabric of family.

Tainted the loyalty of love with the stains of dishonesty.

Stolen the reasons for responsibility by self-fulfillment.

Hardened the hearts of humanity with greed and selfishness.

The content of character is blinded by the rigidity of racism.

Racism which has been perpetrated and perforated onto shades of skin.

Businesses has turned into competitive heartless harassment.

Exhibiting women of wickedness and men of madness.

Idealism replaced by idolatry and livelihood with lust and religious relic.

THE I'S HAVE IT

The essence of the "I" Factor begins with what's important in life.

We first refer to ourselves in the 1ˢᵗ Person, because we value ourselves as most important.

While we marvel those who are intelligent, we deride those who are ignorant.

Women are intuitive and intentional and men are reckless and impulsive.

Children are innovative when their teachers are inspiring.

Our people have become immuned to insanity for fear of being exposed and liable.

When did it become acceptable to sacrifice the innocent and the envolent?

We are in an age where idealism is replaced by self-idolatry.

The modern methods of communication are impacted by idioms rather than veracities.

Our world is currently imploding with irrational inhumanity.

We have been impaled by the endorsement of insidious governments foreign to our founders.

STAID TOO LONG

Too late now to turn back,
To re-do and change your mind.
The reasons why you stayed
Are forgotten and left behind.

Your passiveness got the best of you,
Stalemated and resentful with gloom.
Awaiting a sign to make a move,
The process can't come too soon.

The hateful stares have worn you.
Sharp tongues have torn you down.
How marvelous and bright your smile,
That is now turned upside down.

All the rules and unreasonable demands,
Put forth with such persistence.
But when it's time for your adherence,
They're met with such resistance.

Why require what you can't give?
Why expect the most for less?
Why bow to those beneath you?
Who lick your wounds and hinder success?

If you're assured that the sand,
Is truly softer on the other shore,
Then sail away quietly and quickly
To whomsoever deserves you more.

WE LIVE, WE LONG, WE LOVE

There are those who search the ocean's floor,
Or the sands of hallow ground.
And those who dig in solid earth
For treasures never found.

There are those who steal from others
The things that they don't need.
And sell their souls to quench the thirst,
Of evil and unnecessary greed.

There are those who nurture the seeds of life,
Whether planted or carried by wind.
Who reap and harvest the treasures of life,
And all that nature brings.

For some a life of learning,
And others one of legacy.
We live, we long, we love
Amidst the sky and sea.

DAYBREAK

A Father watches his young son,
Playing innocently with his race cars.
In his exhaustion, he wonders
And awaits the coming of daybreak.
He holds onto each moment of playful joy,
Looking, listening and learning
His son's modes of experience
In the midst of despair and heartache.
Deep within him is the harsh reality,
A world of hate, division and senseless acts.
The judgement of color over character,
That he must one day soon explain.
Coveted injustices enraged with anger,
Masked reneging of constitutional promises.
As the blood of savage racism
Runs fluently in their veins.
As the cars occasionally fall off the track,
His son carefully puts them on again.
He realizes that this act of play
Is a message to fill his own cup.
With patience, prayers and progress.
To strive to build a world of humanity.
For all our children to forever envision
A daybreak of never giving up.

A NEW BEGINNING

Family paths will grow dimmer,
Like the glow from a setting sun
And we won't see what lies ahead
Continuously treading from whence we've come.
We don't know our destination,
Or how long our journey will last.
We can't build love for the future,
Holding malice from the past.
If we engage in turmoil
And submit to those who deceive
Then we have thrown away a lifetime
Of family principles we once believed.
How can we accept each other's death,
If together we can't live?
How can we begin to forget,
If first we can't forgive?
If we can manage the jobs we have
Run households and budget our pay.
Then we can change this family's future
By taking one step today.
If we survive this cruel world daily
An all the sin within it
Then we can strengthen this family bond
Today! Right now! This minute!

SEVEN TWELVE

My spirit is my shelter,
I shall not doubt.
I walk in the paths
Of my ancestors who preparest
A legacy before me.
Yea, though I trod in the streets
Of unrighteousness and unrest,
I will fear no man.
My heritage and wisdom are my
sword and shield.
The quests of yesteryears shall prove
To be victorious and guide me
Through the storms of life.
They regulate my choices of those who have
Kindred spirits and those who seek
To destroy.
And I will bear the fruit of my ancestral spirit,
For as long as I shall live.

A MOTHER'S PROMISE

Mijo,

I carried you under my heart and in my spirit. The one thing I have always asked is for God to protect you, to keep you safe and just.

Even though I long for a simple hug sometimes, I am reminded of a stronger bond between us, when He spared your life twice. Once, He carried you as a baby though a night of influenza, when prayer was the only hope of life for you.

The second time was a night I thought to call but chose to have faith that He would return you safe to me. No one could explain how your car was totaled as it entered the opposite side of the road. He carried though large trees and power poles, landing the wreckage in a small clear space on the grass. For there were no markings of the journey taken.

I pray that you will always honor my faith in prayer and the promise to love you 'til eternity. For you are the greatest gift God has given me.

POSTFACE

Many people have had an influence in my life but not all of them have truly believed that I could become an artist. I was one of few who graduated from high school a year early and had no idea of what I wanted to do in life.

My mother and my aunt made a collaborative effort in guiding my future. In the final hours of closing registration, I submitted my application for admission to Claflin University in Orangeburg, SC. I entered the fine arts program and began my career with twenty-one hours of credit.

Although my teaching career did not include art in the traditional sense, it was successfully used as an enhancement. Poetry, for me is an extension of art. It creates an image, an emotion or an opinion about what is read or heard.

This collection is eclectic and not limited to a particular theme or scheme. Each piece was created at different times and reflects a variety of experiences along this journey called life. I hope it is as inspirational for your reading as it was for my creation.

To my Mother, Eddie Earline Smith Thompson and my Aunt, Georgia Smith Goode.

www.mestrice@stuph.com

CPSIA information can be obtained
at www.ICGtesting.com
Printed in the USA
LVHW040227310322
714849LV00013B/450